CW00345794

Cheshire's Favourite Wildlife

Cheshire

Cheshire's Favourite Wildlife

ISBN 978-0-9572850-0-2

Published by Cheshire Wildlife Trust 2012

Cheshire Wildlife Trust
Bickley Hall Farm, Bickley, Malpas, Cheshire SY14 8EF.

Tel: 01948 820728
www.cheshirewildlifetrust.org.uk

Registered Charity No. 214927. A company Limited by Guarantee.
Registered in England No. 738693

Copyright: The Authors

Designed by MA Creative www.macreative.co.uk
Printed and bound by Gutenberg Press, Malta –
Gutenberg Press prints for Birdlife Malta

*Printed on chlorine-free paper sourced from sustainably
managed forests using vegetable-based inks*

Cheshire's Favourite Wildlife

50 personal stories

Edited by **David Norman**
Photographic Editor **Tom Marshall**

THE
wildlife
TRUSTS
Cheshire

The Wildlife Trusts –
100 years working for wildlife

Cheshire Wildlife Trust is one of 47 individual Wildlife Trusts covering the whole of the UK from Scotland to Alderney. We are all working for an environment rich in wildlife for everyone and have more than 800,000 members including 150,000 members of our junior branch Wildlife Watch.

Our vision is to create A Living Landscape and secure Living Seas. Collectively the Wildlife Trusts manage around 2,300 nature reserves welcoming millions of visitors, and every year advise thousands of landowners and organisations on how to manage their land for wildlife.

We continue to be the UK's leading conservation organisation working locally for the protection of all wildlife and habitats.

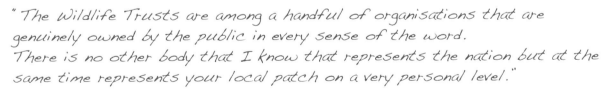

" *The Wildlife Trusts are among a handful of organisations that are genuinely owned by the public in every sense of the word. There is no other body that I know that represents the nation but at the same time represents your local patch on a very personal level.* "

Simon King OBE, President of the Wildlife Trusts

What would you choose?

The idea was simple: Cheshire Wildlife Trust was celebrating its fiftieth anniversary, so let's celebrate the county's wildlife by asking fifty Cheshire people to write about their favourites.

My guidance was brief: up to 200 words (like this Introduction), written in any style. Some replied that they don't really have a favourite, or that they would choose a different species on a different day. But that doesn't matter: this is a selection of stories, and we have chosen some stunning images to match.

Flowers and trees, birds and bees, are all here, with many more and some real surprises. Some are on the doorstep, others are in special places. Some are once-in-a-lifetime experiences; others are seasonal, eagerly anticipated every year, while some are everyday encounters. The message is that there is interest, and joy, to be had in our wildlife wherever, and whenever.

We hope that this collection will entertain, and sometimes amuse; but also that it will captivate, educate, inform and inspire.

David Norman

David Norman, author of Birds in Cheshire and Wirral: a breeding and wintering atlas, was Chairman of Cheshire Wildlife Trust 2004-2012.

Why not tell us about your favourite species?
Send your 200-word text to
favourite@cheshirewt.org.uk.

Your local Wildlife Trust, now and for the future

At Cheshire Wildlife Trust, looking after the region's wildlife and protecting it for the future is at the heart of what we do.

From humble beginnings in the 1960s when the world was waking up to the damage being done to nature, the Trust has now become the leading voice for wildlife in the region at the forefront of landscape-scale conservation. From that very first meeting of like-minded local naturalists through to the latest generation of supporters, our members remain Cheshire Wildlife Trust's foundation.

Today, the Trust brings people closer to nature from the tip of the Wirral to Macclesfield Forest, and on our own wildlife-friendly Bickley Hall Farm in rural Cheshire. We lead projects that have seen the return of species that were once thought lost forever in the region like the dormouse, and manage habitats that provide a home for iconic species like the otter, barn owl and small pearl-bordered fritillary butterfly.

Our reserves network safeguards peat bogs, reedbeds, traditional bluebell woodlands, lowland grasslands and the riverside corridors that form the arteries within an ambitious Living Landscape scheme that will see our most valuable wild places reconnected.

But we don't just do this for the wildlife. We want everyone to enjoy A Living Landscape and that's why you can visit many of our nature reserves for a chance to encounter some of the region's wild creatures for yourself, and why we welcome thousands of young people every year as part of our education programme.

At Cheshire Wildlife Trust we're taking action for wildlife, and if you love Cheshire's wild side we hope you'll want to make a difference too, now and for another fifty years.

Great crested grebe

Chris Mahon

Chris Mahon joined Cheshire
Wildlife Trust in 1994 as
Conservation Manager
and later became Chief
Executive. He now chairs
the International Union
for Conservation of Nature
(IUCN) National Committee
for the UK.

" Look there, on the mere
– over there"

Great crested grebe, icon of conservation
back from the brink of local extinction,
hunted down with guns and traps,
plumage used for fashionable hats.
    Thanks to the work of people who cared,
some who lobbied, some who dared
to challenge the trend and save this bird
   that now is shared and seen and heard.
    "'Look there, on the mere – over there!"
Then gone, hunting below, beak like a spear,
emerging away with a shake of the head,
a cascade of droplets, a fish not quite dead.
    Framed by the edges of Hatch Mere reeds,
courtship gifts of stalks and weeds -
in time, hatchlings riding high,
learning under summer's sky.
    Tunnicliffe then, Ben Hall now,
picture perfect nature's show.
What a beacon for the story
of wildlife's future in all its glory.
    Great crested grebe, icon of conservation,
give us hope for human preservation,
"flagship species" for many reasons ,
teaching people useful lessons.
    You teach your young of nature's bounty,
vanguard the wildlife of our county,
show us the quality of our water ,
should just be here because you ought to!

Tawny owl

Mark Radcliffe

Mark Radcliffe is a broadcaster, writer and musician, regularly heard on BBC Radio 2 and BBC 6 Music, often with his long-term broadcasting partner Stuart Maconie. Mark has lived in Whitley, Cheshire, for a number of years where he enjoys walks among the local wildlife.

I am thrilled to report that my night garden is alive with the screech and chatter of tawny owls. After I put a box in the eaves of a barn and waited patiently, and occasionally impatiently, for a number of years, they have finally deemed it a safe haven and graced us with their presence. Every night at dusk two chicks frolic and chatter in the large sycamore and wait for their mother to return with scraps of food and ready to give them their next flying lesson.

Positioned on a wooden bench by the pond, I then sit motionless and entranced as they take their first tentative exploratory flights between the big tree and a nearby weeping willow. Sometimes they notice me and sit on the electricity wire regarding me with a mixture of nerves and lofty disdain. They quickly head for the cover of the leafy boughs. I can't tell you how thrilled we are to have them. Mind you, if you're lying awake at night unable to sleep their incessant calls don't make dropping off easy.

An iconic elm portrait by David Shepherd dominates our lounge. It reminds me of the vast loss to our landscape in the 1970s and 80s, through Dutch Elm Disease (DED); the associated surge in the disease-carrying elm bark beetles and collapse in the food plant of white-letter hairstreak butterfly.

In 2005 I was surveying woodlands along the Weaver and was thrilled to find an isolated mature wych elm in the corner of a sycamore wood. The Weaver Valley had a substantial elm component, but most succumbed to disease and regrowth is still subject to dieback. So this beautiful tree is a survivor.

Whilst elms continue to suffer a resurgence of disease when they still harbour the fungus in their interconnecting roots, new elms are being successfully planted. Wych elm is preferred as it reproduces from seed rather than from suckers and is less prone to DED.

In the 1980's I was fascinated by the life cycles of the bark beetles and their role in woodland ecology. Now I am nurturing a batch of wych elm grown from seed. Life is coming full circle. In another century perhaps elms will again form skyline trees as noted by Ormerod in his journey across Cheshire 200 years ago.

Wych elm

Joan Fairhurst

Whilst based at Cheshire's Outdoor Education Centre in Delamere Forest, Joan Fairhurst collaborated with her late husband Colin on methods of monitoring and managing Dutch Elm Disease. Since retiring, including from her involvement with Cheshire Watch (The Wildlife Trusts' youth branch), she continues her support of woodland restoration, principally with Trees for Life in the Caledonian Forest.

Dormouse

Sue Tatman

Sue Tatman has worked for Cheshire Wildlife Trust for 15 years, surveying a variety of species including dormice.

"When I first learnt about dormice it seemed a miracle they survived at all"

The dormouse is undeniably cute: those big dark eyes, soft gingery fur, and its general chubby roundness seem designed to appeal. But strangely this charismatic nature is not why I love the dormouse. It's more about how they continue to defy our expectations.

According to the books, the dormouse lives on an ecological knife-edge: confined to a very limited habitat and constantly chasing ephemeral food supplies. When I first learnt about dormice it seemed a miracle they survived at all. But we now know different. It all started when they appeared in nest boxes in a conifer plantation, where all the experts told us they would never survive. Then we heard reports of them raiding bird feeders in gardens, living in hedgerows, and even scurrying across busy roads.

We are finding that dormice are astonishingly well adapted to the life they lead. They are adept at finding new food sources, and can flourish in the most unlikely places. They can adapt their times of sleepiness and wakefulness to suit the vagaries of our climate. This ability to surprise us, to confound the so-called experts, and to demonstrate their fitness to their woodland home, is what I love the most about the dormouse.

Lapwing

Rob Cockbain

Rob Cockbain has been watching birds for over 60 years. He was a founder member of the Merseyside Ringing Group in 1954 and has been instrumental in arranging the conservation of Hale Duck Decoy.

When I was young the lapwing or peewit, with its familiar call and display flight, was known to most people: it was widespread on any wet or damp field, and on almost any field under cultivation. Even a small field could hold several pairs of breeding lapwings. The eggs used to be collected in the spring-time by the locals for food but the birds would quickly lay again and rear young. After the breeding season large flocks would congregate in open fields or wetlands.

During the winter, when the sky was leaden and heavy with snow, large flocks of lapwing would be seen coming into our area of Cheshire having travelled from Eastern Europe to escape the freezing conditions. They would join up with the local birds to form super-flocks of 10,000 birds or more. These would remain until our weather deteriorated and then depart south and west to avoid the snow and frozen ground.

Unfortunately my favourite species is now in trouble: really suffering with our modern farming practices – in particular, autumn planting, the draining of wet and damp areas and the use of nitrates on grassy fields, which kills most of the invertebrates which the lapwings feed upon. Efforts are now being made by various people, including some farmers, to stop the decline of this evocative and beautiful bird.

Whilst surveying the relict dunes on the North Wirral Coast Park at the Gun Site Leasowe for aculeate *Hymenoptera* (bees, wasps and ants) during June 1994 I came across two bees on a south facing dune slope investigating the burrows of the leaf cutter bee *Megachile maritima*. Further examination of the bees revealed them to be the Nationally Scarce cuckoo bees *Coelioxys mandibularis* Nylander.

F. Birch, a member of the Lancashire and Cheshire Entomological Society, found the first British record of this species, represented by a single specimen running up and down a wooden post at Wallasey sandhills on a day in July 1900. Subsequently, Gardiner (1901) found an overlooked specimen in his collection that pre-dated this capture and was collected from the same Wallasey location on 5th July 1891.

Unfortunately little remains of this original habitat and yet, despite intense visitor pressure, often extreme habitat modification and degradation, it is pleasing to record that *Coelioxys mandibularis* can still be found over 100 years later, close to the locations where they were first recorded in Britain.

Cuckoo bee

Carl Clee

Carl Clee is the Cheshire recorder for aculeate *Hymenoptera* (bees, wasps and ants) and since 1994 has been Honorary Curator at World Museum Liverpool.

Robin

Roy Bowden

Roy Bowden has been an active wildlife recorder all his life and brought his skills to Cheshire Wildlife Trust's work, including 12 years as chairman of the Reserves and Technical Committee.

" Not just a fair-weather friend like so many of the other birds, he sticks around through thick and thin"

Don't you just love him? The robin. Wherever you go, he's there singing his beautiful song. Summer and winter; in the woods, in the hedges and especially in the garden, the robin's there. He's so considerate, jumping out from behind the beetroot to rescue worms from my spade; pecking around helpfully, making his contribution. Keeping woodlice out of the compost, keeping an eye on the log pile.

At the feeder, he knows his place. Always happy to bite a passing dunnock, but wary of the sparrow (with his bow and arrow?). First in line for raw pastry, and preferably wholemeal – go easy on the salt. No wonder he's portly. If he's not so keen on anything, like currants, he'll take them off to feed the kids – and come back for more for them. No wonder they've got spots!

Not just a fair-weather friend like so many of the other birds, he sticks around through thick and thin; through rain and snow. Yes, if you've got a robin, every day is Christmas. Our unofficial National Bird: don't you just love him?

Wood horsetail is the daintiest relative of the much-hated field horsetail (often misnamed, even on Gardeners' Question Time as mare's-tail). If you have the latter in your garden, you will know that its roots "go down to Australia" and is very persistent.

The horsetails, *Equisetum*, are survivors of those ancient relatives back in the coal measures and the dinosaur days, when plant reproduction was by spores, and the now dominant seed plants were barely evolving. They are unique in form and some call them "Lego" plants because the stem sections are easily pulled apart. The "weedy" field horsetail must be regarded as the black sheep of the genus, because others of our wild species show the elegance and charm of the form.

Wood horsetail, *E. sylvaticum* is individually, a frail-looking type, recognisable by its branched, downwards curving branches. Best and most typically seen, the many stems merge together to form a bright green ankle-height mist.

In Cheshire, you'd need to go woods or sheltered gullies on the Pennine fringe for the best chance of seeing wood horsetail. It favours damp acid conditions and has survived in these refuges from the march of agriculture and development. Good luck!

Wood horsetail

Liz Blackman

Liz Blackman's love of wildflowers dates from her Westcountry childhood, but she has lived in Sale half her life, where she has been a biological recorder with Cheshire Wildlife Trust's North Group and has led plant identification courses.

Hedgehog

Janel Fone

Dr. Janel Fone is
Chief Executive of
Cheshire Wildlife Trust.

The hedgehog is such a charismatic animal and one that I've had the pleasure to encounter on many occasions – including one curled up inside my son's training shoe in our porch. We evicted him to an overgrown corner of the garden (the hedgehog – not my son), but he turned up again so we put an old training shoe in "The Hedgehog Patch" and that seemed to do the trick!

I admire the hedgehogs' simple approach to defence: any hint of danger and they curl up into a prickly ball until the danger has passed. This served them well for many years, but the last 50 years have seen a massive fall in numbers: from an estimated 30 million in the 1950s to around one million today. Hedgehogs, like much of our wildlife, have been hit by the loss of habitat such as hedgerows and grassland, more intensive agriculture and the use of pesticides. Our gardens are becoming increasingly important for hedgehogs and we can all do our bit by leaving rough, untidy patches to give them a ready supply of insects for food as well as shelter – old training shoes are optional!

"We evicted him to an overgrown corner of the garden - the hedgehog, not my son"

In the breeding season especially, their presence seems woven into the fabric of the River Weaver.

Often by a roaring sluice, or from beneath a soaring sandstone viaduct, the shrill song of a male grey wagtail rings out, when his spring plumage looks most handsome. A riverside nest site is claimed, often hidden within some niche of stone and metal architecture. The pair performs a charming courtship – a choreographed display of almost clockwork precision, and staged appropriately among the marvellous artefacts of Victorian waterways engineering.

With her tail above horizontal, the inviting female crouches with wings lowered and spread slightly in a shivering blur. The sleeked male walks mechanically, proudly presenting his fine black bib, while lowering his wingtips as if to showcase his lengthy tail. Rapid, fanning flicks during exaggerated up and down wags reveal his white outer-tail pattern. He approaches his mate in an almost-stalling hover of shallow flickering wing beats with tail now fanned to full effect.

Later, their young fledge to the sanctuary of nearby oaks, where an inherited rocking 'wagtail' motion betrays rather inelegant, stumpy rear-ends not yet worthy of the name but, with luck, soon to acquire an elegance so characteristic of the adults.

Grey wagtail

David Quinn

David Quinn is a natural history artist and illustrator.

"Their presence seems woven into the fabric of the River Weaver"

Corn poppy

George Osborne

George Osborne has been Member of Parliament for Tatton since 2001; he and his family greatly enjoy walking in the Cheshire countryside.

Papaver rhoeas is the botanical name for the bright red poppy I often see in my Tatton constituency in the Cheshire countryside, flowering beside or in cornfields. Although it generally blooms in late spring, the flowers can appear at any time until the beginning of autumn, owing to the fact that it usually flowers when the soil is disturbed.

It has become a symbol of remembrance because it bloomed in between the trenches during World War I. The famous poem "In Flanders Fields" was written by John McCrae after the death of his friend.

In Flanders fields the poppies blow
Between the crosses, row on row,
That mark our place; and in the sky
The larks, still bravely singing, fly
Scarce heard amid the guns below.

This simple flower, the beautiful red poppy, is now associated with military veterans, especially veterans of World War I. I proudly wear one on Remembrance Day and support the Royal British Legion Poppy Appeal which provides support to personnel and their families, who have served or who are currently serving in the British Armed Forces.

Driving home one evening, I see a white ghost appearing to turn and dip in and out of the headlights as it follows the hedgerow to the left. It was probably a he hunting to feed his she still sitting on eggs. He is living dangerously hunting the margins of this busy country lane.

The barn owl remains a rare bird in the sense that when you see one it is always a special moment. At the nest some hiss and stamp their feet, presenting a fine set of talons in threat; many simply look puzzled and others pretend to be asleep. There is always one that will be determined to draw blood. My blood. A female known to us as 'Lolita' has had two broods by two different chaps in one season and was sleeping around in three different nest boxes!

Owling is never short of interest. The work of the Cheshire Barn Owl groups; talking to landowners and farmers, putting up nest boxes, nest-recording and ringing, continues to ensure an improving population in our county of this charismatic bird.

Barn owl

Bernard Wright
Bernard Wright led the Chester RSPB Local Group and works with barn owls in west Cheshire. In 2006 he was awarded the MBE 'for services to conservation & ornithology'.

"He is living dangerously hunting the margins of this busy country lane"

Mud snail

Dr Mike Tynen

Dr Mike Tynen has worked on aquatic invertebrates at Cheshire Wildlife Trust for the last ten years, following a career spent mainly teaching in further education.

These have been worrying times for anyone concerned about the fate of this vulnerable species of aquatic snail. The winter of 2010-11 was one of unusually low rainfall, and the ditches at Gowy Meadows were dry by May, possibly earlier; and the subsequent months, though cool and cloudy, did not yield significant amounts of rain. Certain of the ditches at Gowy Meadows are home to some of the best populations of mud snail in the Cheshire region, and studies have shown that the main breeding season falls in April or May.

Now, ironically, the mud snail is a species which specialises in seasonally dry habitats. This is what gives it the edge over potentially competing gastropods. Nationally, it is threatened by destruction of its habitat, either by drainage or, conversely, by efforts to make them into permanent water bodies. This year will have been a challenge to its drought-enduring capabilities. Did the populations at Gowy breed before the water vanished? And will those individuals, old or young, alive at the start of the dry period survive until the ditches start to fill again? If the majority have perished, will there be at least pockets of survivors in each ditch, pockets from which the ditches can be repopulated?

I have always admired foxes; I watched one individual sat in the middle of a herd of cows grooming and basking in the summer sun, quietly observing me, and my dogs, from the corner of his eyes but totally unconcerned, as were the cows!

The closest encounters were one particular summer, our dogs were reaching the end of their days and didn't finish their food, a young family of foxes obligingly cleared the leavings away. We would watch from our darkened room, achingly leaning on the window sills for hours, quietly taking photos of the young cubs who were gaining in confidence as they approached our cottage. Their fur dull in the summer's night, lit only by stars and the glow from across the Mersey.

Brave fox – the sorrow and waste of finding one dead creature, minus its tail, left draped over a fence in the coming weeks – left as a warning? As a cynical gesture of disregard for one of our larger wild animals in a country becoming bereft of indigenous species?

To the elegant sleek fox we see regularly – continue please to patrol our fields and make your haunting cry on a winter's night, continue to play and tumble with your cubs in the sunshine.

Fox

Andrew Miller

Andrew Miller was elected as Member of Parliament for Ellesmere Port & Neston in 1992; within his constituency lies Gowy Meadows, the largest of Cheshire Wildlife Trust's Reserves. Andrew has lived in Cheshire for 34 years and enjoys walking through its countryside.

Eyelash fungus

Margaret McCormick

Margaret McCormick, an active member of the Trust's North Group, is passionate about all aspects of wildlife, particularly of her local patch; and can often be found, binoculars, hand-lens and notebook at the ready, out and about on Carrington Moss.

" I left quietly, above me the pigeons applauded, clapping their way out into the nearby fields"

It was late spring, just after dawn and the wood smelled of earth and damp leaves, with a faintly pungent scent of the old dog fox whose earth lay under the roots of the sweet chestnut tree on the southern edge.

Soon my attention was drawn to a fallen birch log, a victim of the winter gales. I could hardly believe my good luck. There, on a cushion of moss lay a small shiny red disc about a centimetre across, edged with a fringe of glossy black hairs. Eyelash fungus *(Scutellinia scutellata)*. I had never seen it before.

The world of fungi fascinates me; it is ephemeral, mysterious and diverse. Some can be eaten, fresh or dried and are nutritious and tasty. Others are poisonous and can be a danger to the unwary gourmet. Excitedly I knelt to take photographs, recorded it in my notebook and paused still kneeling to admire it, for this was no candidate for the pot, no sizzling among the bacon rashers for this little beauty; this specimen was for admiration only.

Oh, how I envied it those luscious dark lashes, so different from my own unremarkable dull brown ones, but my usual bag-lady lifestyle, poking about in woods and hedgerows, does not lend itself to using proprietary aids to allurement, but feminine conceit on this occasion found me gazing wistfully, if only … I left quietly, above me the pigeons applauded, clapping their way out into the nearby fields and another day had begun.

Transcribing bird calls into human sounds is very much an inexact science, but when I was a boy birdwatcher on the Dee estuary, fifty years ago, it seemed to me that the Field Guide (I mean Peterson, Mountfort and Hollom) had very nearly got it right with the redshank: "Usual call," it said, "a musical, down-slurred tleu-hu-hu."

Funny to see it written down baldly like that, in consonants and vowels. Tleu-hu-hu: it could be a verb from an exotic language, though it's actually a pretty accurate description of the sound. But what it doesn't do is convey the shiver it sent down my spine when I heard it drifting across the marshes, this wonderful mournful fluting that pulled together in a second all the beauty of the untouched estuary and the great skies and the distant mountains. Such a handsome bird, too, in flight with its flashing white wing edge, on the ground with its bright orange legs and bill base. Such a pleasure to see. Ah, but the call, the call is the thing, taking me back to the Dee now wherever I hear it, the music of the marshes, seeming to come from the very heart of wildness.

Redshank

Michael McCarthy
Environment Editor for the Independent and author of 'Say Goodbye to the Cuckoo', grew up in Bebington, Wirral and started his birdwatching on the Dee estuary.

"It could be a verb from an exotic language, though it's actually a pretty accurate description of the sound"

White-clawed crayfish

Charlotte Harris

Since leaving University Charlotte Harris has dedicated her career to conservation; engaging people in the natural world and working to protect vulnerable species and habitats. She has worked for Cheshire Wildlife Trust since 2005 and is now Director of Conservation.

My interest in white-clawed crayfish, Britain's only native freshwater crayfish species, was first sparked whilst looking for a suitable subject for my Masters dissertation. At the time I knew little about this charismatic crustacean aside from it being one of our fastest declining animals. Under immense pressure from disease, the invasion of foreign crayfish species and poor water quality, 95% of the UK's white clawed crayfish populations have been lost from all but the cleanest and remotest headwaters. Surprisingly though, and against all odds, they can still be found in some of Cheshire's streams.

Characterised by their lobster-like large front claws, white-clawed crayfish live a secretive life, hiding under rocks and logs during the day, coming out at night to feed on whatever they can find including dead fish, water plants and fallen leaf litter. The females make caring parents, carrying up to 160 eggs on their abdomens over winter. Once the young hatch they cling to their mothers for a further three months before swimming away. The tiny young are extremely vulnerable to predation (even from larger crayfish) and only a handful will survive to adulthood where they can reach sizes of up to 10cm from 'nose' to tail and live for as long as 12 years.

I'll never forget the excitement I felt upon finding my first native crayfish in a Cheshire stream. Only minutes after arriving, I moved a house brick lying in the shadow of a footbridge to see one shoot backwards through the water in alarm. Crayfish add interesting diversity to our watercourses and it is a tragedy that their future is so uncertain. We can only hope that the efforts of conservationists can prevent this endearing species from becoming extinct in the British countryside.

The brimstone is one of the first butterflies I saw on one of my early visits to New Ferry Butterfly Park. Being native to our country it is every bit what I think most people imagine if they were asked to describe a butterfly. Indeed it is said by some that the very description butterfly originates from the yellow colour of male brimstones. For me nothing better encapsulates the feeling of a summer's day than watching these delicate and most attractive of insects go about gathering their food.

Although I suspect the cooler summers of recent years will not have been helpful to butterflies the fact that examples of the beautiful brimstone butterfly can be found in a greater number of locations across northern England in recent years will, in part, be due to the excellent work being done by members of Cheshire Wildlife Trust and supporters of urban nature reserves such as the butterfly park in New Ferry.

The park not only offers a haven for butterflies but it is also a valuable addition to the local community, providing as it does much-needed opportunities for recreation and for local school children to learn about the natural environment. I hope the brimstone will thrive at the park and, along with the twenty-plus other species of butterfly that share the site, will continue to enhance our lives for a long time to come.

Brimstone butterfly

Alison McGovern

Alison McGovern was born and grew up in Wirral South and was elected MP for the constituency in 2010. She is pleased to live a few minutes' walk from New Ferry Butterfly Park.

Swift

Brian Martin

Brian Martin organised
the county-wide survey of
swifts in Cheshire and Wirral
in the mid-1990s, having
been passionate about the
species for as long as he can
remember; he has swifts
breeding on his house and
continues to be involved with
Action for Swifts, a national
group dedicated to their
conservation.

*"The finest flyers,
dashing and screaming
above our towns and
villages"*

For some, spring arrives with the first swallow or the plaintive song of the willow warbler. For me, however, it is the return of the swifts in early May which raises my spirits most. These all-black birds with sickle-shaped narrow wings are one of the finest flyers, dashing and screaming above our towns and villages on warm summer evenings – one of the great uplifting sights of nature!

Swifts are long-lived birds and build their nests in roof spaces or nooks and crannies in older buildings. They feed on flying insects and the food balls they bring back can contain thousands. This reliance on insects leads to problems in inclement weather, but the young are adapted to go into a semi-torpid state when food is scarce.

The swift's stay is all too brief and by August many are already heading south. Sadly, they have experienced a major fall in numbers in recent years from a loss of nest sites due to insensitive roof repairs. Swift enthusiasts are working hard to halt this decline. They must succeed for how sad it would be to look to the sky in spring and not be able to shout "They're back!"

The silver birch is one of the most familiar and easily recognised of the trees native to Britain. Known also as the "Queen of the Woods", its silvery-white bark and pendulous brownish twigs brighten up winter days. Cheshire also has the downy birch which has bark not as bright as the silver birch. Both species are excellent pioneers, producing masses of small wind-dispersed seeds. The silver birch is more a tree of light soils whilst the downy birch is found on wetter sites and moorland. Both can be in the same area and the hybrids they produce can cause confusion.

When the fresh green foliage appears in April it brings back many happy memories of looking for my first willow warbler of the year amongst the birch scrub. As spring progressed I would find my largest concentrations of breeding pairs due to the abundant supply of caterpillars in the birch woodlands.

With the approach of autumn the birch wood is a very pleasant sight as the leaves turn to a pale yellow. Autumn is also the period when the cones ripen, attracting flocks of siskins and redpolls feeding on the abundant seed crop in the trees, and later on the ground when the seed has fallen.

Birch

Jack Swan

After training at Edinburgh's Royal Botanic Garden, Jack Swan was involved managing woodland nature reserves and woodland planting including the management and development of the Jodrell Bank Arboretum for 23 years; he has a lifelong interest in birds from dwelling in the countryside with access to excellent woodland and riparian habitats.

Spotted flycatcher

Richard Blindell

Richard Blindell has studied the birds of eastern Cheshire for 34 years, and is currently researching the breeding success of Peak District waders, particularly lapwings.

One of my favourite paintings is that of a spotted flycatcher, given to me by friend and Essex artist R.P. Hull. He had difficulty selling it; such a relatively nondescript species, hard to locate and certainly under-recorded, was perhaps not sexy enough for his clientele.

But not for me; the bird is evocative of the best times of year: May-time, with hedgerows bursting with blossom and warbler-song, alongside flowery, buttercup-filled meadows, and summer gardens and country churchyards, with towering lime trees under azure, cumulo-nimbused skies.

It is a bird of the full flush of spring, arriving shortly after my other favourites, lesser whitethroat and garden warbler, and presenting an immediate challenge to the birder, singing its indistinct song from deep within the canopy and confusing the listener with its ventriloquism and its mimicry of juvenile robins.

The bird is subtle in voice and plumage, but less so in behaviour, when characteristically fly-catching, and when family parties forage in the open along fruity hedgerows as summer wanes. A connoisseur's bird, perhaps not as scarce as its "amber listing" might suggest, at least not along northern river valleys and Cheshire's Peak District fringes.

Walking in woodland and listening to birdsong. Suddenly my senses are swamped by the scent of bluebells wafted on the damp breeze. Taking me back to my childhood and walks with my parents when we'd come home, our arms full of spring. Running around the house in search of any receptacle: short enough, and water tight, to display their slender nodding blue stems.

Of course I'm talking about the English bluebell *(Hyacinthoides non-scripta)* and of a time when it was plentiful and we didn't know that picking them was one of the worst things we could do. Now we spread the message to everyone not to pick, but to enjoy them in their natural habitat. Breathe in their sweet scent after spring showers in native woodlands – where they belong!

Even though it still faces many other threats – including loss of its native habitat and cross-fertilisation with the Spanish bluebell – the native English bluebell does not have a national Biodiversity Action Plan (BAP) for protection. However, the dedicated members of the Cheshire Bluebell BAP Group have a shared passion: the aim is that it will remain – as found in a 2002 nationwide survey by Flora Locale – Britain's favourite wild flower.

English bluebell

Paul Oldfield

Paul Oldfield is a member of the Cheshire Bluebell Biodiversity Action Plan (BAP) Group, now in its second decade of working to save the English bluebell.

"Taking me back to my childhood and walks with my parents when we'd come home, our arms full of spring"

Sand martin

Peter Walton

Peter Walton is the only
remaining founder-subscriber
of Cheshire Wildlife Trust,
and Bollin Valley sand
martins are among the many
birds celebrated in his poetry.

Forgetting that the martins nested there,
we wander up a local valley – past the weir,
The busy road bridge, and the cattle fields
where slick spring pasture already yields
aside to comb a parting for the path.
The river keeps its opposing pace, with
constant never-repeated travel talk,
as we tire and look to pause our walk
before the turn for home.

And it's here,
above the low-browed river cliffs just more
than our head-height, we see the wheeling birds,
hear gravel voices and Saharan words
from these survivors of vast journeying.
I count to thirty burrows, with burrowing
still going on where birds have made first dints
in sand and stones. They swerve away – sky-prints
of swift-winged butterflies – then back
to their own cuts of cliff, with the one-track
minds of returning brave riparians.

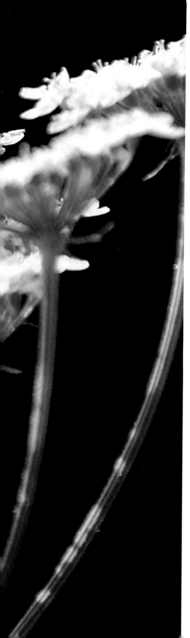

Since I became interested in butterflies a few years ago I have been fascinated by the hairstreaks. As treetop butterflies they are a real challenge to see and study. The white-letter hairstreak is a particular favourite because it survives despite the major loss of elm trees – its caterpillar's foodplant. It's not a particularly beautiful or colourful butterfly and the plain brown upperwings are never seen but it's a survivor and I love it!

Generally the hairstreaks keep in the treetops feeding on aphid honeydew but occasionally they will descend to nectar on thistle or bramble. In 2010 I spent a lovely morning trying to get my first photographs on the sunny side of a hedge with a couple of elms but with a good patch of bramble in flower at the base. After a long wait a white-letter hairstreak came down to the bramble and I could enjoy the fine detail of its underwing and get some photos – perfect! The butterfly stayed for over an hour and was still there when I reluctantly left it to get home for lunch.

White-letter hairstreak

Neil Friswell

Neil Friswell is a trustee of Cheshire Wildlife Trust, chairs the Trust's Conservation Committee and is passionate about conservation of the county's wildlife.

Dipper

Ben Hall

Ben Hall, Cheshire born and bred, has provided many images for Cheshire Wildlife Trust publications from his website **benhallphoto.com**. In 2011 he became the Trust's newest – and youngest – Vice President.

" I will never tire of watching one bob under the fast flowing water, seemingly running along the river bed"

Being a wildlife photographer specialising in capturing images of animals in their habitat, I find myself constantly drawn to those species that live in particularly beautiful surroundings. The dipper is one such bird.

It is certainly not a flashy character, its plump appearance and dreary brown and white colours are not the reason I dedicate hours and hours to photographing it, but rather the beautiful environments which it inhabits. Spending time near crystal-clear streams and babbling brooks make photographing this bird a pleasure. I will never tire of watching one bob under the fast flowing water, seemingly running along the river bed completely submerged, searching for tasty morsels amongst the rocks.

Although some of my best-selling images are of dippers, I will never feel like my work is complete. Each image is different just as each bird is different, and this is one of the reasons I can be found time after time, crouching in the bushes beside a Cheshire stream watching and photographing this beautiful yet unassuming bird.

Western sea-lavender

Eric Greenwood

Eric Greenwood spent most of his professional life at the Liverpool Museum (now World Museum, Liverpool), where he was in charge of the museum's collections. On retirement he was able to spend more time on his life-time study of North Lancashire's flora, culminating in 2012 with the publication of his book Flora of North Lancashire.

Hilbre at the mouth of the Dee estuary is home to one of Cheshire's rarest plants. It is also one of its most attractive with mauve-coloured flowers. Near relatives are great favourites of flower arrangers.

The plants on Hilbre belong to a group called rock sea-lavenders and are found on rocky coasts and at the top of pebble beaches and stony salt marshes in southern and western England and Wales. Whilst individual populations are all similar to each other there is considerable variation between them. This is because over a long period of time each population or group has evolved slightly differently. Our plants belong to a group extending from Anglesey to southern Cumbria and are found nowhere else in the world. They are endemic to the region.

The populations of *Limonium britannicum ssp. celticum* are frequently small and often decreasing. There used to be several colonies on the Wyre and Lune estuaries in Lancashire but today it has gone from the Lune estuary and the number of colonies on the Wyre is much reduced.

However it is a plant that responds to conservation measures. By the 1970s the Hilbre colony was close to extinction but measures were implemented to protect the remaining plants. These proved successful and the colony expanded. Nevertheless it needs continuing careful protection if this special Cheshire species is to survive.

Bullhead

James Baggaley

James Baggaley began
his nature conservation
work in Cheshire with
rECOrd before moving
into Local Government;
he is now Principal Nature
Conservation Officer with
Cheshire East Council.

*"To me, as a child,
lifting up stones in a
small brook was the
key to another world"*

Being flat, big-headed, spiny, goggle-eyed and habitually spending most of the day hiding under stones are not the characteristics that you might normally associate with anybody's favourite species. But that's the bullhead (also known as Miller's Thumb) and it's mine.

The appeal of the species perhaps becomes more obvious when you learn that the males care for their eggs by fanning them to ensure they are oxygenated and safe from fungal infection. Bullheads also sing (well at least grunt and growl) to attract females. They are resilient little fish surviving the last Ice Age in glacial refuges, challenging the view that all fish species arrived in the UK after the retreat of the ice.

To me, as a child, bending down and lifting up stones in a small brook was the key to another world. Staring down into the glare of clear water, amongst other treasures such as caddis fly larvae and the occasional brook lamprey, I found the bullhead looking more like something that belonged in a rock pool than its preferred habitat of tree-lined, rocky streams with well developed ripple and pool structure.

The bullhead is quite widespread in England and Wales but has an unfavourable conservation status across Europe, being listed on Annex II of the EU Habitats Directive, with Special Areas of Conservation (SAC) designated for the species. There are no such SACs in Cheshire, but we are fortunate that this fascinating creature can be found in most of the waters in the county.

Snowdrop

Our favourite snowdrop was first found at Heawood Hall near Nether Alderley in the 1890's by Sir Graeme Elphinstone. It was named Lady Elphinstone by the famous galanthophile Samuel Arnott.

Like all snowdrops she is a harbinger of spring and weathers snow and sharp frosts by bowing her head and jumping up again when temperatures rise, unscathed and still beautiful. The hardiness of this species is an important attribute when opening the garden at Rode in February for snowdrop walks.

No predator dares to eat Lady Elphinstone as snowdrops contain a poison, Galantamine, a compound that shows promise in treating Alzheimer's. The ancient Greeks knew this; Odysseus was given a bulb by Hermes to counteract the intoxicating nerve drugs that Circe used to induce amnesia. It would be fanciful to speculate that if there had been no snowdrop bulb or moly as the Gods called it on board for the crew there would have been no Odyssey! Certainly Lady Elphinstone has a very romantic past!

This Cheshire snowdrop which is a double, is different from any other *Galanthus* hybrid in that some years she turns yellow and in others she turns green and no one knows why. It is to be hoped that Sir Graeme's wife did not do the same!

Richard and Anne Baker Wilbraham

Sir Richard, who retired as President of Cheshire Wildlife Trust in January 2011, and Lady Anne Baker Wilbraham, both keen galanthophiles, live at Rode Hall which has been the Wilbraham family home since 1669.

Cuckoo

Charles Hull

Charles Hull is the British Trust for Ornithology's voluntary Regional Representative for South Cheshire and is involved in monitoring the population changes of our local birds.

"A sign that spring has at last arrived"

The song of the cuckoo is recognised by most people even if they have little interest in wildlife; it is a sign that spring has at last arrived. However in the last few years the number of cuckoos heard in Cheshire has fallen dramatically and it has become a very rare breeding bird in the county. Conservationists are studying why this might be:

Breeding – is there a shortage of host birds? In Cheshire most cuckoos lay their eggs in nests of dunnocks or meadow pipits, both now species of conservation concern as their numbers have declined.

Food – cuckoo chicks eat whatever insect-food their foster-parents give them, but, once independent, cuckoos especially feed on large hairy caterpillars of various moth species, unpalatable to most other birds. Many of us can recall night-time road journeys when our windscreens became covered with moths, but those are distant memories now.

Migration – cuckoos winter south of the Sahara Desert but we know little about them once they leave our shores. Recent exciting results from birds being satellite-tracked by the British Trust for Ornithology (BTO) will help targetted conservation action on their migratory routes and in Africa.

Climate – cuckoo numbers have actually increased in Scotland and Ireland: is it now too warm for 'our' birds in Cheshire?

As well as supporting the bird organisations studying their decline, we can all help by passing on records of Cheshire cuckoos whenever we find them, and enjoy them whilst we may.

Bee orchid

Sarah Bird

Sarah Bird is the Biodiversity Officer at Chester Zoo and grew up in Alderley Edge (before the footballers moved in).

" I became a back-seat botanist, counting the spikes of orchids from the car"

The orchid pages of my childhood flower book were the most thumbed, and finding a 'new' orchid thrilled me. I became a back-seat botanist and would count the spikes of hybrid spotted orchids on the embankment around the Altrincham runway tunnel from the car. By my teens I was somewhat blasé about 'common' orchids, however, one real gem still eluded me. It is, I believe, the most beautiful of the UK's wildflowers... *Ophrys apifera* – the bee orchid.

In 1980 I chose a book on Orchids of Britain and Europe as a school prize. *O. apifera* was still top of my wish list. The book said it was quite common – definitely found in Cheshire – but elusive, taking over five years to mature and flower. Frustration! It seemed I was always in the wrong place at the wrong time.

And then in 2000 I finally found bee orchids... first at Pickering's Pasture in Halton, and then, near Northwich, in Cheshire at last! My most memorable bee orchid experiences are a wonderful French meadow with more than 30 blooms seen with Cheshire Mammal Group, and very recently finding them at Chester Zoo in the Jaguar enclosure and the main car park in 2011. I think I have a sixth sense for these orchids and for this last one I just got the feeling that there was something interesting there from a glimpse in the corner of my eye whilst driving home one evening – and went back the following day...

Now I aim to see this lovely species every year.

At first sight this may seem like a strange choice. Surely there are more interesting creatures in the county than a common hawker *(Aeshna juncea)*. Well, like many English vernacular names, 'common' is entirely inappropriate in most parts of England, including Cheshire. In his 'Dragonflies of Europe', K-D Dijkstra suggests 'moorland hawker'. Now you're talking.

So why choose *Aeshna juncea*? For six years I carried out a study of the odonata (dragonflies and damselflies) at a site known as Handforth Fields, in the far north of the county. Whilst the odonata diversity was very good for a single site, there were none of the rare or exciting Cheshire species present. *Juncea* was the crème de la crème at this site.

However, it shouldn't really have been there. Moorland, as far as we're concerned means acid habitat, but the water pH at Handforth was 7.85. OK, that's only marginally alkali, but *juncea* likes less than 6.0. So it was a surprise to first locate these insects, then to see them breeding (egg-laying females).

Finally, if you can manage to see males at perch, they are actually very attractive, as is their behaviour. Watching them hawking for food, or earnestly searching for a female, for minutes on end is, for me, a real joy.

Common hawker

Stu Burnet
Stu Burnet is a former birder and a self-taught naturalist, now with a foot in many camps, though these don't include centipedes! With a leaning towards sun-loving insects, he is an active wildlife conservationist, and a lay officer with Butterfly Conservation.

" Watching them earnestly searching for a female, for minutes on end, is a real joy"

Yellowhammer

Helen Carey

Helen Carey is a former Council member of Cheshire Wildlife Trust and the daughter of the Trust's second Chairman, Philip J Askey, a keen ornithologist who was fortunate enough to go bird watching for many years with A W Boyd.

"All is right with the world and I feel happy"

This bright, cheery-looking bird is my favourite for many reasons. Perched on my thick hawthorn hedge they seem indomitable, singing in the winter sun and bringing colour and music to my life and my garden.

Looking out of my kitchen window on a late winter morning I see several bright yellow birds feeding on the ground and breathe a sigh of relief. Thank goodness the yellowhammers are still around! Spring must be on the way. All is right with the world and I feel happy – what a sustaining and joyful sight they are.

Standing in our garden in Weaverham, when we were children, my twin sister and I would try and listen attentively while our father would explain to us which bird sang which song. The yellowhammer's *"little bit of bread and no cheese"* was unmistakeable.

But for how much longer will we hear that song? I am fortunate to live down a country lane, bounded by farmland and surrounded by birds and birdsong. But sadly these farmland and hedgerow birds have seriously declined over the past 25 years and are on the Red List species of high conservation concern.

Here they come! As the tide goes out the black-tailed godwits fly in from their roost onto the mud at Thurstaston. They start feeding as soon as they land, far too hungry after a freezing night to be bothered by a strange man staring at them from just a few yards away. Numbers soon build up and I estimate well over a thousand. Then suddenly they start 'talking', the whole flock quietly twittering as they walk slowly towards me; a magical moment.

In the air they are black and white, but as soon as they land the black and white wings and tail are hidden from view and they turn into a uniform grey. Nevertheless, I see the occasional flash of colour. These are colour rings which about one in a hundred have on their legs. I first note six birds which are regulars here; it is like seeing the return of old friends. Then I am thrilled to see two 'new' ones. From the ring combination I reckon they were ringed in Iceland. I go home happy, content that the reporting of these rings to 'Operation Godwit' will contribute to the migration studies of this charismatic species.

Black-tailed godwit

Richard Smith

Richard Smith edited the Cheshire and Wirral Bird Report 2005-2011 and runs the Dee Estuary Birding website **deeestuary.co.uk**.

Magnolia

Viscount Ashbrook

Michael Ashbrook is a Vice-President of Cheshire Wildlife Trust. He and his family have imported and cultivated Magnolias at Arley Hall for more than two centuries, so they surely deserve to be considered a Cheshire species!

Magnolia must surely rank as one of the most outstanding genera hardy in the British climate and in terms of flowering trees it is almost unsurpassed. The hybrid *M. x soulangeana* is very familiar in April in town and country. Equally well known is *M. stellata*, smaller and sometimes easier to place, since many magnolias achieve an enormous size as any one who has seen them in Cornish gardens will testify. At Arley we have a number of the very large Asiatic varieties, in particular *M. campbellii* subsp. *mollicommata* and *M. sprengeri* 'Diva' which, if not affected by spring frosts, produce huge saucer shaped flowers in white or varying shades of pink.

One of my most unforgettable experiences trekking in Nepal some years ago was rounding a corner in woodland and finding an enormous magnolia covered in white blooms. On the whole magnolias are easy to please, tolerant of most soil conditions and fast growing, though some beautiful varieties native to the USA such as the evergreen *M. grandiflora* and *M. macrophylla*, which I believe has the largest leaves of any tree hardy in the temperate world, are more tender.

The Dee Estuary is the most important wintering site for this graceful, streamlined duck in the UK and is of international importance.

They arrive from their northern breeding grounds in the early autumn. At low water they tend to loaf in large tight flocks hugging the channels between Oakenholt and Bagillt on the Flintshire side of the estuary. On incoming high tides they fly in to feed along the edge of the saltmarsh on the Cheshire side and gather in huge flocks, up-ending to reach the rich source of seeds on which to feed. During spring tides in the autumn they will take flight to overnight roosts and for me, one of the most amazing bird spectacles on the estuary is to be standing on Burton Point in late autumn in the early evening light and watch squadron after squadron of pintail arriving in from the estuary to the RSPB reserve at Burton Mere Wetlands.

They come in very high over Burton Marsh presumably to avoid the wildfowlers' guns and then drop down in a spectacular fashion onto the pools to roost. On one evening I counted an incredible 3,500 birds and No1 pool was covered in a thick carpet of these beautiful ducks seeking refuge on the reserve – a sight which will stay with me forever.

Pintail

Colin Wells
Colin Wells has been manager of the RSPB's Dee Estuary sites since 1984 and can see the flights of pintail from his office window.

"The pool was covered in a thick carpet of these beautiful ducks"

Desert wheatear

Hugh Pulsford

Hugh Pulsford has been a keen birdwatcher all his life, is a licensed ringer and is currently County bird Recorder for Cheshire and Wirral.

" It is ridiculously out of place, both in time and space, yet somehow it appears completely at home"

Picture a grey mid December morning framing a somewhat surreal background, twelve foot steel razor wire topped fencing, with security cameras and flood lights surrounding stark brick warehousing beside a tangle of rail tracks that make up the National Rail's Freeport at Crewe. Ignoring wagons and forklift trucks, darting amongst the plastic covered goods on pallets, is a vision in yellow and black; a bandit-masked plump desert wheatear.

It should have been in arid habitats of North Africa or the Middle East, but somehow, it's here in Cheshire, a waif and stray of bird migration. It sallies back and forth from wooden perches as it flits from tarmac to stacked pallets, flashing its white rump, and black tail, its black wings delicately marked with pale fringes. An orangey yellow back and crown top a black face cut by a bold white stripe through its eye. It is ridiculously out of place, both in time and space, a lost vagrant, yet somehow it appears completely at home. Alerted by a worker to its presence, this is a private site and I am alone, and privileged to be allowed to enjoy this first for Cheshire and Wirral, a birding moment *par excellence*.

Twenty-ninth of May
Royal Oak Day
If you don't give us a holiday
We'll all run away

Oak

Growing up in a Shropshire village near to Boscobel, home of a descendant of the great oak tree Charles II hid in after the Battle of Worcester, this rhyme was part of my childhood. Wearing an oak apple and leaf on May 29th, we demanded a half-day holiday.

Oak trees are part of our Cheshire landscape. Looking across the Cheshire Plain from Kelsall Hill to the Dee and Mersey, the sturdy oak dominates. They are part of our heritage. How many of us have sung "Hearts of Oak" with a feeling of pride in our naval heritage and visited historic buildings held up by huge oak beams?

Individual oak trees can produce 9,000 acorns a year and the 'Marton Oak', in East Cheshire, aged at least 1,200 years and said to be the largest sessile oak in Britain, is still producing a good crop.

The trees are home to birds, mammals, amphibians, reptiles, fungi and lichens. Beetles, woodlice, butterflies and moths make their home in oak trees. Surely, oak trees can truly be said to demonstrate biodiversity in a microcosm.

John Gittins

John W. Gittins is a geographer. He has worked in Cheshire for over 25 years latterly for the unique Cheshire Landscape Trust. Currently he is working with Dr. Clemency Fisher on a biography of A.W. Boyd, the great Cheshire naturalist.

Kingfisher

Stephen O'Brien

Stephen O'Brien has been MP for Eddisbury since 1999, and is pleased to have the headquarters of Cheshire Wildlife Trust in his constituency, both in their former home at Grebe House and in the present Bickley Hall Farm.

" Wonderfully designed by nature and absolutely honed for its purpose"

My favourite species is the kingfisher: so rarely glimpsed only as a flash of startling aquamarine, a kingfisher is striking and a creature of beauty. Wonderfully designed by nature and absolutely honed for its purpose, both flying and diving, to spot one not only raises the spirits but it reminds me of the sheer splendour of our spectacular countryside in Eddisbury and the never-ending wonders of the natural world.

Club-tailed dragonfly

Being responsible for Cheshire's odonata (dragonfly and damselfly) records in the 1980s, I met the national recorder, Bob Merritt. He had found club-tailed dragonflies on the river Severn and wondered, as their headwaters are quite close to each other in the Welsh hills, if the species might ever have crossed to the river Dee. So, on the sunny morning of 8 June 1985, Bob and I, with Pip Adams, started walking up the bank of the Dee although, at his request, on the Welsh side of the river.

I will never forget the moment when Pip calmly said "I've got one". She had found the first club-tailed dragonfly exuvia (the shed larval skin) on the river – the farthest north in Britain – the adult characteristically having emerged within the dry mud of a cow's footprint. If I could have walked across the water into Cheshire I would have done so, but it took a 16-mile detour and a couple of hours combing the eastern bank before we found our first county exuvia.

A year later I was entertaining the Gloucestershire recorder Sonia Holland to a whistle-stop tour of our main dragonfly sites and went to the Dee on the off-chance. We parked at the end of a track near Caldecott, walked down to the river and, almost immediately, found the first ever Cheshire adult club-tailed dragonfly, a teneral (recently-emerged) male still with its milky wings. Again the excitement was intense and she stayed 'guarding' it whilst I rushed back to the car for my camera, only to be met by an irate farmer as I was blocking his tractor. Thankfully the dragonfly hadn't flown by the time I returned, and was duly captured on film for posterity.

Today I find it so satisfying to know that the range and numbers of this charismatic dragonfly on the Dee are increasing.

Richard Gabb

Richard Gabb has always been keen on flying creatures; for a number of years he edited the Cheshire and Wirral Ornithological Society's Bird News magazine and he co-authored the Dragonflies and Damselflies of Cheshire, published in 1992.

Who would not marvel when seeing the kestrel focussed on its prey, stationary in a buffeting wind? Gerard Manley Hopkins captures this miraculous feat:

The Windhover

I caught this morning morning's minion,
kingdom of daylight's dauphin,
dapple-dawn-drawn Falcon,
in his riding

Of the rolling level underneath him steady air, and striding
High there, how he rung upon the rein of a wimpling wing
In his ecstasy! Then off, off forth on swing,
As a skate's heel sweeps smooth on a bow-bend: the hurl and gliding
Rebuffed the big wind. My heart in hiding
Stirred for a bird, – the achieve of, the mastery of the thing.

Kestrel

The Duke of Westminster
KG CB OBE TD CD DL
The Duke of Westminster became Patron of Cheshire Wildlife Trust in January 2011.

Yellow rattle

Joe Winstanley

Joe Winstanley has been providing environmental advice to farmers and landowners in Cheshire for over 10 years and since 2005 has run his own consultancy Agri-Environment Advice Ltd. Joe has a particular interest in the management and restoration of species-rich and wet grasslands.

There will be few people reading this who are unaware of the lamentable loss of species-rich grassland in Britain during the last 60 years and that Cheshire has suffered heavier losses than most counties.

Clearly nothing can ever replace the conservation value of ancient unimproved grassland, but I believe we should always do our best to restore or recreate species-rich grasslands where such opportunity exists, not least to leave some reminder to future generations of how things once were.

Now, re-creating and restoring species-rich grassland is no easy task, however the conservationist wishing to restore a hay meadow has a very useful ally in a plant that is perhaps easy to overlook.

Also known as hay rattle, due to the characteristic rattling of the fruit within the bladder, which was said to indicate the meadow being ready for harvest, the plant is something of a Robin Hood in the plant world. Its hemi-parasitic qualities allow the plant to weaken the vigour of the aggressive grasses, which in turn creates space for more delicate grasses and wildflowers and there is also some suggestion that yellow rattle can influence soil conditions to benefit other wildflower species.

So there we have it, yellow rattle may not possess the intricate beauty of the bee orchid, the brilliant colouration of great burnet or the evolutionary brilliance of sundew but to those concerned with restoring meadows it provides invaluable assistance: at a time when British wildlife has never been under greater pressure, we need all the help we can get.

Whilst visiting the many corners of Cheshire over the last ten years a particular highlight of mine was finding singing skylarks in an unexpected location, set between industrial units, car showrooms and vacant plots. Although more commonly associated with open farmland the skylark seems at ease in areas of land long since cleared of its previous use but with no immediate future, known to you and me as brownfield land or to give it its technical term 'OMHPDL' (Open Mosaic Habitats on Previously Developed Land).

Its uplifting song is still discernable, fighting against the background of road traffic and overhead aircraft, and is an escape from the modern world of emails and pdfs. Who knows what the artistic Shelley and Hardy would say.

It is shame that few will hear its voice as they are cocooned in a car or a lorry. Will it survive in this new urban home – why not? The ever changing landscape of economic growth and downturn appears to mimic the rise and fall of the lark.

Skylark

Alun Evans

Alun Evans has worked across Cheshire for over ten years and is currently Principal Biodiversity Officer with Cheshire West and Chester Council. The views expressed here are his own.

" Its uplifting song is still discernable, fighting against the background of road traffic and overhead aircraft"

The stinkhorn

Eric Fletcher

Eric Fletcher grew up learning about wildlife in Cheshire and North Wales, and is now manager of rECOrd, the county's biodiversity information system.

" More often hidden out of sight, but the smell was always there".

For me the stinkhorn has to be one of my favourite species and is truly, to my mind, synonymous with damp woodland. I feel its charm comes from the strong odour you encounter long before seeing it, that is if you are lucky enough in scrambling around to try and find it.

My first experience of the stinkhorn was during what some might say was a misspent youth, exploring every inch of woodland surrounding the village I grew up in. In particular there was a clough woodland that was a mix of plantation and broadleaved that seemed, when I think back now, to always have a fresh stinkhorn, more often hidden out of sight, but the smell was always there.

Some years later and I had the privilege of attending a fungus identification course where we came across a stinkhorn that had very recently distributed its spores, courtesy of various invertebrates. We were then informed that the smell given off by the stinkhorn is chemically identical to that given off by hyacinths, a message that has stuck with me ever since.

Amidst all the negative stories about the environment, the buzzard is a welcome reminder of what conservation can achieve. Forty years ago a Cheshire birdwatcher would have had to cross the border into Wales to be guaranteed of seeing this majestic predator, but now buzzards are a familiar resident throughout our county. Their spread has been achieved through policy changes in agricultural management and species protection, hard won by scientists and conservationists.

Greater familiarity has never diminished the excitement that I feel when seeing one of these impressive birds of prey soaring over the Cheshire Plain or sitting menacingly on a fence post at the side of a road. Paradoxically, their bullying demeanour belies a lazy side as they tend to seek out carrion in preference to hunting live prey and you can also see them on ploughed fields hunting for earthworms and other invertebrates. Globally they are widespread and I often see them on my conservation-related visits to other parts of the world, but my favourite encounters of buzzards are in Cheshire, wheeling around above the familiar landscape, their mewing cries mocking the environmental pessimists and spurring me on to work harder for wildlife.

Buzzard

Simon Dowell

Simon Dowell is a lecturer in Conservation Ecology at Liverpool John Moores University, a Conservation Fellow and Trustee at Chester Zoo and a former Trustee of the Cheshire Wildlife Trust. His conservation work for the Zoo has concentrated on protecting forests for endemic birds in China, but he frequently draws his inspiration from watching birds in and around his home on the edge of the Cheshire Plain.

Chaffinch

Paul Mackenzie

Paul Mackenzie is Deputy Editor of *Cheshire Life*.

" The trousers were warm from the washing machine and therefore a cosy place to perch"

My first published work appeared in a bird magazine when I was six years old. I wrote to ask why birds visiting our garden would perch on my school trousers on the washing line. The answer I was given, that the trousers were warm from the washing machine and therefore a cosy place to perch, intrigued me and I spent the next week's pocket money on a bird book.

It was a pocket sized guide, with a watercolour of a chaffinch on the front and a space to put a triumphant tick beside each bird once you had spotted it. Looking back now at the number of golden eagles I claimed to have seen, I'm not sure I was entirely honest in my marking, but from the moment I bought it I was entranced by the chaffinch on the front.

Its rich colours, inquisitive cocked head and the better than average chance of spotting one appealed to me and even now the sight, or the cheery sound of one never fails to lift my spirits.

"Believe me, my young friend", said Ratty to Mole, "there is nothing – absolute nothing – half so much worth doing as simply messing about in boats. Simply messing". In 'The Wind in the Willows', when the stoats and weasels threatened to disrupt riverbank life, Ratty took up arms and in a famous battle saw them off. In real life, it's a different story.

'Ratty' is a water vole and no match for that vicious foreign invader, the American mink. For me, 'Ratty' is the quintessential symbol of our native wildlife's struggle for survival.

In the UK, 90% of water voles have disappeared over the past 20 years but in Cheshire and Lancashire, Ratty is back! Trust volunteers declared war on the mink and that other enemy, pollution. Mink have been forcibly removed from rivers, habitat restored, and pollution cleaned up.

Ratty is once more messing about in Frodsham, Warrington, Lindow Common and Lancashire's River Wyre where, for the first time in years, I saw that portly little bundle of fur and whiskers busily rooting about the river bank a foot from where I was sitting.

With that familiar 'plop', Ratty was off, a small victor in the fight to save our wildlife for future generations.

Water vole

Felicity Goodey

Felicity Goodey has enjoyed watching wildlife as relaxation during her busy career in the media, regeneration and business. She became President of Cheshire Wildlife Trust in January 2011.

"With that familiar 'plop', Ratty was off, a small victor in the fight to save our wildlife for future generations"

White stars spread across the woodland floor! For me, spring has really "sprung" when the wood anemones come out. One glimpse of them shining in the April sunshine, mixed with the yellow of celandines, and I ditch the paperwork for a visit to Dibbinsdale Woods. You may know them as "windflowers", after the way the deceptively fragile blooms dance in the spring breeze. This is a species of ancient woodland, one of the many reasons to cherish our remaining woodlands. It sets little seed, and that short-lived, so it is very slow to spread to new habitats.

Where established, it spreads by underground stems, so each patch is one plant, as shown by the occasional pink-flowered group. The local bees and hoverflies appreciate the flowers, judging by the number to be seen visiting them where the sunlight strikes through the leafless trees. A very good excuse for sitting quiet and watching. Thirty years ago, when I first came to Wirral, the anemones came out at the end of April. Now it is usually two weeks earlier. Climate change is real – what are you doing to lessen its impact?

Wood anemone

Hilary Ash

Hilary Ash is a botanist and for more than 20 years has been Honorary Conservation Officer for Wirral Wildlife (the Wirral Group of Cheshire Wildlife Trust).

"White stars spread across the woodland floor!"

Prior to starting to work with the Cheshire Wildlife Trust in 1987, I made an exploratory visit to Marbury Country Park (where the Trust was based at the time) and ventured to nearby Neumann's Flash.

As a newcomer to Cheshire I didn't even know the site was called Neumann's Flash, I just found it whilst driving back to Northwich. This was to be my introduction to what became a love-affair (some may say an obsession) with the area. It wasn't long before I saw a wader on the water's edge, taking off and giving its characteristic trisyllabic twit-wit-wit. Immediately I knew I was watching a green sandpiper and it soon alighted a little further away and continued to feed, occasionally bobbing. Scanning round I saw about a dozen of these waders.

Regular visitors to the Witton area will know that this is not unknown, especially in July and August, but to me it was quite a surprise. Even now 25 years later, I still get a thrill when I hear a green sandpiper; to some a chiffchaff is the first sound of spring, but to me a green sandpiper calling from a flooded field in July heralds the start of the return autumn wader passage, whilst the occasional overwintering one reminds me that spring is just around the corner!

Green sandpiper

Paul Hill
Paul Hill chairs the Cheshire Region Biological Records Centre (rECOrd) and is active in recording as much Cheshire wildlife as he can, as a volunteer and with his own environmental consultancy.

Weasel

Jacki Hulse

Jacki Hulse is a Land Manager with Cheshire Wildlife Trust, who feels privileged to have been involved in the management of private estate land and nature reserves throughout her working life.

" He moved so fast that it was impossible to distinguish where his head began and his tail finished"

This beguiling, elusive, determined creature, common in our countryside but seldom seen, has enthralled me for years.

I have seen weasel on a number of occasions; on many I have only glimpsed them, but once I was lucky enough to be sitting in a vehicle eating my lunch at the head of a green lane. A female appeared from long grass on the edge of the lane, sat up on her haunches, turned left then right along the track. She then proceeded across the pathway. Seconds later she returned to the original side, waited for a brief moment and then headed across the track with three kits in a line behind her.

This behaviour is believed to be the origin of one of the many collective nouns for weasel; gang. Kits can kill prey at eight weeks old and this rapid development led people to believe gangs of adult weasels went about the countryside rather than family groups.

Phil Drabble had a tame weasel called Teasy who he described as 'a sprite… a golden leaf on the tongue of a whirlwind'; he also said 'He moved so fast that it was impossible to distinguish where his head began and his tail finished'.

Sanderling

Dashing along the tide-line, making sudden sallies, legs churning like clockwork toys, a group of sanderling on the shore is always a delight to see.

Although sanderling breed only in the high Arctic region, they are characteristic of British shores in winter, and non-breeding flocks can be found at almost any time of the year. Unlike most wading birds, this is a confiding species which often allows quite a close approach, when its silvery plumage and dark legs can be fully appreciated. The backs of juvenile birds are very beautifully patterned. A quaint characteristic, which distinguishes the species from other sandpipers and stints, is the lack of a hind toe.

A small flock encountered on the beach will fly before you with soft 'twick-twick' calls, soon settling again not far ahead. In strong winds they are blown and buffeted as they run helter-skelter along the beach deftly avoiding the breaking waves.

Breeding in the Siberian and Canadian Arctic, and in Greenland, this is a truly northern species, yet in winter it can range as far as southern Asia, western America, West Africa, and even Australia. But Britain's winter population is the largest in Europe, and indeed it appears very much at home on our Cheshire estuarine shores.

Stuart Crooks

Stuart Crooks was a founder member of the Hertfordshire & Middlesex Wildlife Trust, before becoming, in 1972, Cheshire Wildlife Trust's first Conservation Officer. In 1978 he moved to Lincolnshire Wildlife Trust, eventually becoming Director. Stuart's lifetime of service to the Wildlife Trust movement was recognised in 2008 by the award of the Cadbury Medal.

Acknowledgements

Thanks must go to all the authors who kindly gave us their thoughts and memories of the wildlife that is special to them, from the iconic to the often underrated creatures and plants that make up the natural world on our doorstep.

However, this varied and often intriguing collection simply would not catch the eye without the images that accompany those memories. We are hugely grateful to the many photographers who have supported this project with their striking work, capturing the very essence of the natural world as we see it, from keen amateurs to some of our leading nature photographers. Thanks to Damian Waters who did some of the initial work on finding suitable images.

You can find photographic credits on the following pages, including the websites of many of the contributors.

Photography

Small pearl-bordered fritillary – **Nigel Kiteley**

Simon King – **Marguerite Smits van Oyen**

Yellowhammer
Chris Grady
wildlife-imaging.co.uk

Silver Jubilee Bridge
Alan James

Grey Seal
Neil Aldridge

Dormouse
Tom Marshall

Trentabank Reservoir
George Bayode

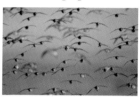

Dunlin
Ryan Askren

Brown hawker
Matt Cole

Great crested grebe
Ben Hall
benhallphoto.com

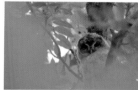

Tawny owl
Lindsay Macrae

Wych elm
Alan Gregg

Dormouse
Danny Green
dannygreenphotography.com

Lapwing
Tony House

Cuckoo bee
Tony Emmett

Robin
Paul Bunyard
wildaboutimages.co.uk

Wood horsetail
Niall Benvie
naturepl.com

Hedgehog
Ben Hall
benhallphoto.com

Grey wagtail
David Quinn
davidquinnwildlifeart.co.uk

Corn poppy
Mark Hamblin
markhamblin.com

Barn owl
Paul Bunyard
wildaboutimages.co.uk

Mud snail
Roy Anderson

Fox
Jon Hawkins
surreyhillsphotography.co.uk

Eyelash fungus
Herman Giethoom

Redshank
Steven Dugdale

White-clawed crayfish
Robert Thompson
naturepl.com

Brimstone butterfly
Matt Berry
greenwings.co

Swift
Ernie Janes
naturepl.com

Birch
Mark Hamblin
markhamblin.com

Spotted flycatcher
Richard Steel

Bluebell
Damian Waters
drumimages.co.uk

Sand martin
Duncan Cooke
happydayzcards.com

White-letter hairstreak
Tim Melling

Dipper
Ben Hall
benhallphoto.com

Western sea-lavender
Tricia Gibson

Bullhead
Simon Colmer
naturepl.com

Snowdrop
Amy Lewis

Cuckoo
Mark Hamblin
markhamblin.com

Bee orchid
Ross Hoddinott
rosshoddinott.co.uk

Cheshire's Favourite Wildlife

Common hawker
Phil Corley

Yellowhammer
Chris Grady
wildlife-imaging.co.uk

Black-tailed godwit
Peter Warne

Magnolia
Michael Ashbrook

Pintail
Chris Grady
wildlife-imaging.co.uk

Desert wheatear
Mark Caunt
markcauntphotography.com

Oak
Amy Lewis

Kingfisher
Malcolm Brown

Club-tailed dragonfly
Phil Corley

Kestrel
Paul Bunyard
wildaboutimages.co.uk

Yellow rattle
Ian Worsley

Skylark
Richard Steel

Stinkhorn
Nicholas Armitt
nicholasarmittphotography.com

Buzzard
Mark Davison

Chaffinch
Mark Hamblin
markhamblin.com

Water vole
Tom Marshall

Wood anemone
Ross Hoddinott
rosshoddinott.co.uk

Green sandpiper
Eduardo Bologh

Weasel
David Tipling
naturepl.com

Sanderling
Andrew Malcom